FRICTION
ALL
AROUND

FRICTION
ALL AROUND

by
TILLIE S. PINE
JOSEPH LEVINE

Illustrated by BERNICE MYERS

Also by Tillie S. Pine and Joseph Levine

THE INDIANS KNEW

THE PILGRIMS KNEW

THE CHINESE KNEW

MAGNETS AND HOW TO USE THEM

SOUNDS ALL AROUND

WATER ALL AROUND

AIR ALL AROUND

Library of Congress Catalog Card Number: 60-14224
Published by Whittlesey House
A division of the McGraw-Hill Book Company, Inc.

Second Printing

Are you in your house?
Look around you.

Is Father striking a match?

Is Mother scouring a pot?

Is someone scraping his feet
on the doormat?

5

Are you outdoors?
Look around you.
Is a street-cleaning truck sweeping the street
with its turning brushes?
Are men pushing a heavy box
along the sidewalk?
Is a car stopping suddenly?

Are you in school?
Look around you.

Is your teacher writing on the blackboard?

Are you erasing a number on your paper?

Is someone sandpapering a piece of wood?

Wherever you are,
indoors or outdoors,
you see things rubbing
against each other.

Do you ever rub one thing
against another?
Of course you do.
When you

write or draw,

walk or run,

slide or slip,

and even—
when you turn this page!
So you see—
all around you
things are rubbing.
And—
when things are rubbing
we have
FRICTION.

WHAT MAKES THINGS WEAR AWAY?

Crayons get short.
Tires get smooth.
Rugs get thin.
Soles get holes.

Do you know why these things happen?
You can do some simple things to find out.

Look at the rubbing side of a piece of sandpaper.

Feel it. Is it rough? Yes, it is.

Rub the piece of sandpaper against the side of your pencil.

What do you see?

You see that some of the wood is worn away where you have rubbed.

You also see tiny pieces of the wood that you have rubbed away.

What makes this happen?

The rough sandpaper rubs against the wood and tears away tiny pieces of the wood.

Now do this:

Look at a nail file.

Feel it.   Are the flat sides rough?

They surely are.

File your finger nail.

What do you see?

You see that your nail is worn down where you file.

You also see tiny pieces of your nail that you have rubbed away.

What makes this happen?

The rough nail file rubs against your nail and tears away tiny pieces of the nail.

When rough things rub, they wear away.

What happens when smooth things rub?
Try this.

Rub your finger on a new piece of chalk.
Smooth, isn't it?

Rub your finger on the blackboard.
Quite smooth, isn't it?

Now write your name on the blackboard,
then—
look at the tip of your chalk.

Is it worn away?   It certainly is.

Your name on the blackboard
has the worn-away chalk.

So—

even when smooth things are rubbing
they, too, wear away.

Why?

If you could look at smooth things
through a strong magnifying glass,
you would be surprised to see that
smooth things are really not smooth—
they have tiny bumps on them.

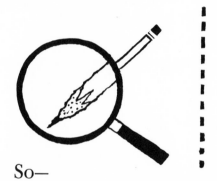

So—

when smooth things rub, some of these tiny
bumps are worn away.

Now you know that—
when rough things rub they wear away;
when smooth things rub they, too,
wear away.

When things are rubbing
we have friction.

And—
friction wears down crayons, tires,
rugs, and shoes.

13

Look at each picture carefully.

What thing is rubbing against another thing?

What do you think is wearing away more in each picture?

We have friction when things rub.

And—
friction makes things wear down
and wear away.

Sometimes there is only a little bit of wearing away with friction.

And—

sometimes there is a large amount of wearing away with friction.

What can you do to see this?

Rub a new crayon lightly across a piece of paper.

Look at the tip of the crayon. What do you see?

You see that very, very little of the crayon is worn away.

Now—

rub another new crayon heavily across the paper.

Look at the tip. What do you see?

You see that much more of the crayon is worn away this time.

When you rub lightly, only a little bit of the crayon wears away because there is little friction.

But—

when you rub heavily, more of the crayon wears away because there is more friction.

Now try this.

Sandpaper a piece of wood, first lightly, then heavily.

What happens when you rub lightly?

What happens when you rub heavily?

The easier the rubbing, the less the friction.

The less the friction, the less the wearing away.

And—

the harder the rubbing, the more the friction.

The more the friction, the more the wearing away.

Who wear things away in their work?

The floor-scraper does—

   when he scrapes floors.

The scissors-grinder does—

   when he sharpens scissors.

And—

you wear things away when you—

   file your nails,

   and—

   erase pencil marks.

DOES FRICTION MAKE THINGS HOT?

Men who cut down big trees
stop sawing every once in a while.
Do you know why?
They want to rest from their hard work,
of course.
But—
they also stop sawing for another reason.

Do this and you will see what the
reason is.
Get a long nail. Feel its tip.
It feels cool, doesn't it?

Now—
rub the tip of the nail quickly, back and forth
on the sidewalk for a few times.

Feel the tip again.

Does it feel warm? It surely does.

What makes the tip warm?

The rubbing does.

When things are rubbing, we have friction.

And—
friction makes heat!

The lumbermen know this.

They stop sawing because they understand
that the saw rubs and rubs as it cuts
into the tree.

The rubbing makes the saw hot,
so hot that it expands a little
and sticks in the cut.

The men cannot saw.

The heated saw might also break.

So—the men
stop sawing to let the saw cool off.

Do you know how to keep warm
outdoors in cold weather?

Of course you do.

You wear warm clothing.

But—

do you know how to use friction
to help you keep warm?

Rub the palms of your hands
together lightly.

Do they feel warm?   Yes, they do.

Now—

rub the palms of your hands together harder.

Do they feel hot?   They certainly do.

So you see—

you can use friction to help you
keep warm in cold weather.

And—

the easier you rub, the less the friction.

The less the friction, the less the heat

But—

the harder you rub, the more the friction.

The more the friction, the more the heat.

Sometimes friction can make things
so hot that sparks fly.

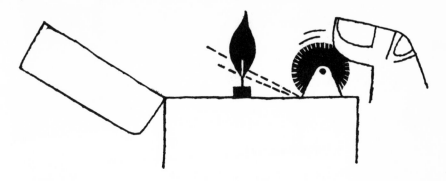

Father turns the wheel of his
cigarette lighter. The wheel rubs against
the flint quickly. Tiny pieces of flint wear away.
The rubbing makes them hot—
so hot that they burn, and—
   sparks fly!
   Train wheels roll over steel tracks.
The wheels rub against them. Tiny pieces of steel
wear away. The rubbing makes them hot—
so hot that they burn and—
   sparks fly!

Grindstones spin as knives are sharpened.
The grindstones rub against the steel knives.
Tiny pieces of the steel wear away.
The rubbing makes them hot—
so hot that they burn and—
   sparks fly!
   Sometimes friction can make things
hot enough to start a fire.
   Boy scouts know this.
   They spin the tip of a long stick
against another piece of wood. They are using
the Indian drill. The rubbing makes wood-dust
which gets hot—so hot that it begins to burn.
   The boy scouts use this small flame
to light their campfires.

Sometimes friction can make things
so very hot that they can burn up.

Jet planes roar through the air
very, very fast.

As they fly, they rub against the air.

The faster they fly, the more they rub.

The more they rub, the hotter the planes get—
so hot—that they *could* burn up.

But—
the builders of these planes know this.

They build these jet planes of special
materials that will *not* burn up, no matter
how fast the jets fly through the air.

A rocket is shot high, high into space.
It travels higher and higher—
so high that it flies past the air around the earth.
   Then the nose cone of the rocket
begins to fall back to earth.
   When it comes back into the air, it falls
faster and faster—
so fast that it gets hot by rubbing against the air—
so hot that it *could* burn up.
   But—
the builders of rockets know this.
   They build the nose cones of special materials
that will *not* burn up, no matter how fast
rockets travel through the air.

High, high in space small pieces
of stone are flying around.

Sometimes some of these stones
fly into the air around the earth.

They fly faster and faster and they get
hotter and hotter as they rub against the air—
so hot that they glow and burn up.

We call these glowing stones *meteors*.

Sometimes some of these meteors
do not burn up completely. They hit the earth
and cool off.

Then we call them *meteorites*.

Did you ever imagine that rubbing
could make so much heat?

DO WE WANT THINGS TO SLIDE AND SLIP?

Do you know—
  why Mother puts a rough rubber mat
in the bathtub?
  Why batters tape the handles
of their bats?
  Why violinists put rosin
on their bows?
  You can find out why by doing
a simple activity.

Rub the smooth sides of two pieces
of sandpaper together.

Do the papers slide easily
over each other? Yes, they do.

Now—
rub the rough sides of the pieces
of sandpaper together.

Do they now slide easily
over each other? No, they do not.

When you rub the smooth sides
together, the papers slide easily,

because—
there is little friction.

When you rub the rough sides
together, they do not slide easily,
because—
there is much friction.

So you see—
the less the friction, the easier the sliding,
and—
the more the friction, the harder the sliding.

Sometimes we *want* the rubbing parts
of things to be smooth, because we *want*
moving things to slide easily.

We make a smooth pole
in the firehouse so that the firemen
can slide down easily.

We want smooth ice for ice skating.

We want snow-covered hills
for sleigh riding.

We make smooth sliding-ponds
in playgrounds.

We make smooth chutes
to slide coal from trucks to cellars.

Sometimes we *want* the rubbing
parts to be *rough*, because we *want*
to slow down or stop things
from sliding or slipping.

We put rough rubber mats in bathtubs
to keep people from slipping
in the smooth tubs.

We put sand on icy roads
to keep cars from slipping and skidding.
Sand makes the smooth ice rougher.
This keeps turning tires from slipping
and skidding on the ice.

We tape the handles of bats
to keep the bats from slipping out of the hands
of the batters when they swing at the ball.

We see violinists rub rosin
on their bows to keep the bows
from slipping on the strings as they play.

WHEN DOES TURNING AND SPINNING HELP US?

People all over the world have always
moved heavy things from place to place.
And—
they found ways of making this work
easier and easier.
You can find out for yourself
what these ways are.

Fill your school bag with books.
Lay the heavy bag on the floor and slide it
across the room.   Does it move easily?
No, it does not.
Now—
put three or four round sticks or pencils
on the floor. Lay them in a row, one in front
of the other.
Place your heavy school bag
on the sticks and pull it.
Does it move easier this time?
It certainly does.

Why is it hard to move the bag
the first time and easy the second time?
    When you slide the bag along
the floor, the whole side of the bag
touches the floor and rubs against it.
    There is much friction.
    But—
when you pull your bag over the sticks,
it moves over rollers.
    There is very little sliding
    and—
there is less friction.
    The more the friction, the harder the moving.
    The less the friction, the easier the moving.
    Now do you see that
people found out
they could roll things instead of sliding them
to make their work easier?

There is another way to make it
still easier to move things.

Do this:

Put your heavy school bag
on your toy cart.

Push your cart. Watch how easily
the bag moves across the room.

What helps you this time?

The wheels on the cart do, of course!

Do you know how the wheels help?

Move your toy cart slowly across the floor.
Watch the wheels roll.

There is almost no sliding as the wheels roll.

And—

because there is almost no sliding,
rolling wheels make very little friction.

Therefore the cart moves very easily.

Now do you see that people
found out wheels could help them
make their work easier?
Where do we use wheels to make work easy?
We use wheels
on wheelbarrows and carts,
on wagons and trains,
on cars and trucks,
on bicycles and motorcycles.
We even put wheels on furniture legs.

Long, long ago, when people used
wheeled carts and wagons, they soon
found out something very important.

The wheels squeaked and groaned.
They turned slowly and wore away too soon.

What made these things happen?

Friction did.

How?

The wheels turned on axles and rubbed
and rubbed against them. The rubbing
made the squeaking, the groaning, and
the wearing away.

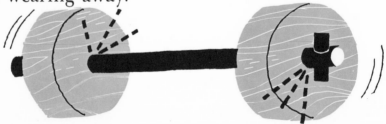

What did the people do to make
the friction less?

Do this and you will find out:
Hold one end of a round pencil
tightly in your fist.

Turn the pencil with your other hand.
It is *hard* to do, isn't it?

Now—
rub a little Vaseline on the part
of the pencil that you grasp.

Hold the greased part of your pencil tightly.
Turn the pencil again.
It is *easy* to do now, isn't it?
Why?

The Vaseline fills in the tiny spaces between
the tiny bumps of the smooth pencil.
It also fills in the tiny spaces
in the bumps of your smooth palm.

This makes the pencil and your palm
smoother than before.

And so—
there is less friction between the pencil and
your hand.

The pencil slides around more easily
in your hand as you turn it.

Do you see why people put grease
on the axles?

The grease made the wheels turn easily—
without squeaking, without groaning,
and without quickly wearing away.

Today—
we put oil or grease on turning wheels.
We put oil in motors.
We grease automobiles.
We oil door hinges,
   and—
you oil your skate wheels.

So you see—
because oil and grease help to make less friction,
things turn and spin very, very easily,
and very, very smoothly.

There is another way to make wheels
spin still more easily.

Look at your roller skates.   Spin the wheels.
Do you see how easily and quickly they turn?
Do you know why?
Do this and you will know:
Put a small piepan into a larger pot.
Spin the small pan in the pot.
What happens?
It does not spin easily.
Why?
The bottom of the pan slides
and rubs against the pot.
There is much friction.
Now do this.
Take out the piepan.
Put a dozen round beads or marbles
in the pot.
Put the small pan on the beads
and spin it!
Surprised?
The pan spins very easily this time.
The bottom of the piepan touches
and rubs only on the beads.
There is less friction.

Now look at your skate wheels again.
Do you see the small steel balls
in the wheels?
We call these—*ball bearings*.
The wheels roll around on these
ball bearings and turn easily and quickly.
Where do we use ball bearings
to help wheels turn very easily?
We use ball bearings in—
    bicycle wheels,
    train wheels,
    car wheels,
    truck wheels,
    and in—
    motors of all kinds!

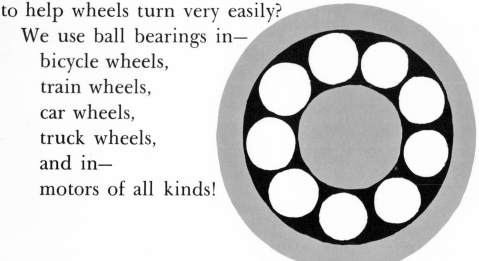

Now you know that there is less friction
when things roll than when things slide.
So—
we use wheels to help us move things
more easily and much faster.

HOW CAN WE MAKE ELECTRICITY
BY RUBBING?

Do you remember when you slid across the seat of your father's car, touched the handle and—
Crack!
You felt a sharp tingle in your fingers.
Do you know what made this happen?
You can easily find out!
On a clear, cool day, slide your feet across a rug.
Then—
touch something made of metal— a door knob, a tray or a pot.
Do you feel the tingle?
Do you hear the crackle?
Do you see the spark?

When you rub your shoes
across the rug, there is friction. This makes
a special kind of electricity on your skin.
We call this electricity "staying electricity,"
or "static electricity."

When you touch the metal,
this "staying electricity" jumps from you
to the metal. It becomes "moving electricity."

This makes—
the tingle you feel,
the crackle you hear,
    and—
the spark you sometimes see.

So—
the sharp tingle you felt when you
slid across the seat of the car
was static electricity that jumped from you
to the handle of the door.

Where else can you see static
electricity jump from one thing to another?

Some scientists believe that
high in the air, millions
and millions of tiny drops of water
in storm clouds rub against the air.

This rubbing makes more and more
static electricity in the clouds.

Sometimes this electricity jumps
from one cloud to another.

Sometimes it jumps from the clouds
to the earth.

When these things happen, static
electricity becomes moving electricity,
and—
you see a huge spark.

This huge spark is *lightning!*

You can have fun with static electricity.

Put some tiny pieces of tissue paper into a low, clear, plastic box which you can look through. Close the cover,

and—

rub your fingers several times across the box.

Are you surprised to see that the papers jump up and stick to the cover?

Now—

rub the top of the box.

Rub the bottom of the box.

Watch the pieces jump around.

Have fun making the papers jump and stick, jump and stick.

What makes this happen?

When you rub, you make static electricity in the box. This rubbing makes enough static electricity to make the papers jump and stick.

Now—

blow up a toy balloon.   Tie its neck.

Place it against the wall and take your
hand away.   Does the balloon stick to the wall?

It does not!

Rub the blown-up balloon with a piece
of woolen cloth or fur.

Place it against the wall again
and take your hand away.

Does the balloon stick to the wall
this time?   It certainly does.
Static electricity makes it stick.

Now do this.

Touch your comb to a piece of thread.

Does the thread stick to the comb?
It does not.

Run your comb through your hair
and touch the thread again.

What happens now?

The thread jumps to the comb
and sticks to it.   Static electricity
makes it stick.

Try this:

Place a sheet of paper flat against
a large mirror and take your hand away.

Does the paper stick to the mirror?

No, it falls down!

Place the paper flat against
the mirror again.

But, this time—
rub the paper, back and forth,
with the palm of your hand.

Take your hand away.

Does the paper stick to the glass?
Yes, it does.

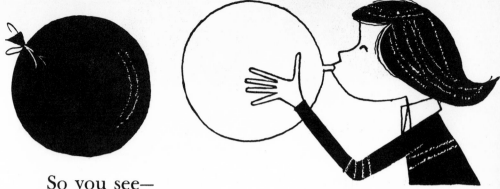

So you see—
you can rub *different* things together
to make enough static electricity and make
them stick.

But—
sometimes you can use static electricity
to make things do something else.

Blow up two balloons. Attach a string
to each balloon.

Ask a friend to hold both strings
so that both balloons hang down and touch
each other.

Now—
rub each balloon with a piece of woolen cloth
or fur.

Are you surprised to see
the balloons push away
from each other?

The static electricity in each balloon
makes this happen.

Now do this.

Take a long sheet of writing paper.
Tear it in half, the long way.

Lay each strip of paper on a woolen cloth.

Rub each paper, the same way, several times.

Hold both strips of paper together at one end.

What do you see?

You see the other ends of the paper
push away from each other.

Now you know that
you can rub things made of the *same*
material to make enough static electricity
to make them push away from each other!
    So—
friction makes static electricity.
    And—
static electricity—
    makes sparks,
    makes things move,
    makes things stick to each other,
    and sometimes—
    makes things push away from each other.

Did you ever imagine
when you looked around—
   in the house,
   outdoors,
   in school,
that friction could do so many
different things?

531
P

copy 2